A STEP-BY-STEP BOOK ABOUT
CANARIES

ANMARIE BARRIE

Photographs: Dr. Herbert R. Axelrod; Leslie Arnall; Patricia Demko; Michael Gilroy; Harry V. Lacey; Donald Perez; Mervin F. Roberts; courtesy of Vogelpark Walsrode.
Humorous illustrations by Andy Prendimano.

Distributed in the UNITED STATES by T.F.H. Publications, Inc., 211 West Sylvania Avenue, Neptune City, NJ 07753; in CANADA to the Pet Trade by H & L Pet Supplies Inc., 27 Kingston Crescent, Kitchener, Ontario N2B 2T6; Rolf C. Hagen Ltd., 3225 Sartelon Street, Montreal 382 Quebec; in CANADA to the Book Trade by Macmillan of Canada (A Division of Canada Publishing Corporation), 164 Commander Boulevard, Agincourt, Ontario M1S 3C7; in ENGLAND by T.F.H. Publications Limited, 4 Kier Park, Ascot, Berkshire SL5 7DS; in AUSTRALIA AND THE SOUTH PACIFIC by T.F.H. (Australia) Pty. Ltd., Box 149, Brookvale 2100 N.S.W., Australia; in NEW ZEALAND by Ross Haines & Son, Ltd., 18 Monmouth Street, Grey Lynn, Auckland 2, New Zealand; in SINGAPORE AND MALAYSIA by MPH Distributors (S) Pte., Ltd., 601 Sims Drive, #03/07/21, Singapore 1438; in the PHILIPPINES by Bio-Research, 5 Lippay Street, San Lorenzo Village, Makati Rizal; in SOUTH AFRICA by Multipet Pty. Ltd., 30 Turners Avenue, Durban 4001. Published by T.F.H. Publications, Inc. Manufactured in the United States of America by T.F.H. Publications, Inc.

Contents

Canaries were originally found on a few temperate islands in the Atlantic Ocean. They are natives of the Canary Islands off the African coast, and of Madeira and the Azores by Portugal and Spain. The little birds live in parklands, fruit farms, and on slopes with little vegetation. They feed on seeding plants—crucifers and composites, notably cabbage and lettuce, as well as poppy, chickweed, millet and others. Very popular is canary grass, of which "canary seed" is an important component of every canary food.

INTRODUCTION

In February and March, canaries begin nest building. They are tree-dwellers, and their nests can be found near the outer end of the branches.

In the wild, canaries are grayish-green or greenish-yellow. The sexes differ slightly in color and markings. The male is a deep green, with yellow on the head and yellow-green on the upper tail coverts and rump. Overall, the female is more grayish in color, with fewer yellow-green markings.

Selective breeding has fixed the type, colors, and song of the domestic canary. Although they are not mutually exclusive, there are generally considered to be three categories of canaries.

The Roller canary has been bred for song; its appearance is not important. The song is like a trill or roll, delivered with a closed beak. What the bird sings with an open beak is considered of an inferior quality.

The Color Bred or Red Factor canaries are bred mainly for color, though they are still respected for their song. These canaries come in a great variety of colors, from deep orange to

FACING PAGE:
Domesticated canaries of this color bear a
considerable resemblance to their wild ancestors.

light red, yellow, white, pink, and green. The more red in the plumage, the more expensive the bird. Certain shades of red can be enhanced by foods and dyes.

The other type canaries are bred for special characteristics, such as size or an unusual shape. They are typically named for the area in which they were developed. These include the Norwich, Yorkshires, Border Fancy, Dutch Frill and Gloster Fancy. The Lizard canary is named for its distinctive color pattern.

Of course, all male canaries sing no matter what category they belong to. Male color canaries sing, but their song is not as intricate and structured as that of a Roller which has been subject to selective breeding for song over generations. Conversely, color breeders have devoted their efforts to beauty; song was not taken into consideration. Therefore, the song of a color bird is less cultivated, and its song may be loud and shrill. All male canaries sing, and a few female canaries have

The Yorkshire canary is bred for a particular "type," which includes an upright stance and considerable size.

been known to sing a little, but not a really continuous song. It is more like a warble.

Canaries are well-suited to life in captivity. They are rugged, docile and long-lived, having life spans of up to twenty years. Canaries are attractive and come in a wide variety of colors. They require minimum space and a simple diet. Canaries

Besides color, canary breeds—like the Border and the Fife Fancies shown here—also differ in size.

have good personalities and great singing abilities which provide an enjoyable source of entertainment. Canaries also pose no harm to children or strangers.

Little upkeep is required in taking care of canaries. A few minutes is needed each day to replenish food and water, and once a week the cage needs to be thoroughly cleaned. The

A prize-winning Border canary in its show cage. With show canaries, as with other animals, superior specimens command higher prices.

necessary food and equipment are inexpensive. This ease of care and low cost make canaries good pets for beginners learning the basics of birds.

Of course, there are some disadvantages to be considered when purchasing a canary. Canaries are susceptible to drafts and sensitive to changes in their diet. The cage must be kept clean, and the bird should be allowed to fly for exercise. Unfortunately, there are no records of a canary being housebroken, so droppings may be found throughout the flying area.

Canaries can be left alone two or three days with

The Norwich is one of the largest canary breeds. This specimen shows the feather texture known as "buff," which is characterized by light edging.

proper food and water. If an extended trip is planned, a reliable friend needs to visit every other day to care for the bird. A canary, though, is easily transported to another location for supervision.

Canaries do sing beautifully, but they are not known to imitate a human voice or other sounds. They are not capable of advanced tricks, either. A parrot would be better suited for these purposes.

If you plan to breed your canary at home, it can be accomplished. Other types of caged birds are more willing to breed and more easily reared, though.

Canaries are timid birds. It is not wise to house them with hooked-beaked birds that may be more aggressive. If a canary is attacked, it could be severely harmed.

The care and feeding of canaries is not expensive or time consuming. They are an ideal pet in living quarters that can not accommodate other small domestic animals, and it is easy to find other bird enthusiasts. Local bird clubs and shows are located in many areas.

Canaries with so-called variegated markings show patches of dark and light color in their plumage.

SELECTION

A variety of stores sell birds. Choose a pet shop or bird store with experienced, reliable employees. Seek out sales people that know how to handle the birds and can offer sound advice. They are the ones to rely on for help in selecting a bird and all the proper equipment. The dealer should have a good inventory of food and supplies so that everything can be bought in one place. Inspect the cages. They should be clean and neat, important for insuring a healthy bird.

Fall is the best time to look for a canary. By November or December, the breeding period is well over. The moult is complete and the birds will be showing their true plumage. The singers will be in song, and the young will have matured. Prices will be reasonable because there is a larger number of young and older birds in stock.

The most important criterion is to choose a healthy bird. A canary should be sleek and well-groomed, with full plumage. No bare spots should be seen. Avoid a bird with ruffled feathers or watery eyes and nostrils. Rather, the canary should be bright-eyed, alert, and inquisitive. Stand back from the cage to avoid interfering with natural behavior, and observe the bird for as long as possible. It should display an active interest in its food and be lively when moving about the cage. Note any prolonged periods of lethargy or motionless. A puffed-up and tired look can mean the bird is sleepy, but it can also be a sign of illness.

Handle the canary in the store and thoroughly examine it. It will be anywhere from 4 ¾–8″ in length. The breast should feel firm, plump, and full. The bone should not stick out or feel sharp. If the chest area is reddish- blue or the intestines

FACING PAGE:
Tidy plumage, along with liveliness and alertness,
are indicators of a health canary.

are visible as dark lines on the stomach, the bird needs to be passed over. While holding the bird, it may seem that the canary vibrates, as if it were a tiny motor. This is because of the high metabolic rate of canaries. What you are feeling is the heart beating.

Look for damaged or dirty feathers. The entire body should be clean, not soiled, including the vent region. Loose, watery droppings will stick to the feathers, indicating diarrhea. The droppings in the cage must be a mixture of black and white

A canary nestling about to fledge shows a well-formed bill and feathers that are not yet fully opened.

or grayish brown, not yellow or green. Do not accept a bird with sores or wounds.

The canary's mandibles should come together nicely and not be overgrown or deformed.

If you are planning to tame the bird, buy only one. Additional birds will be more interested in each other and therefore harder to tame. If you want two birds, do not pair up two males. Since they are dominant, fierce fighting may occur and the birds may be harmed. Females are not as apt to fight, but they are not likely to sing, either. So if buying one of each sex, they can be kept together for most of the year, but must be separated for the two months prior to the breeding season. Probably the best idea if you want to keep more than one bird is to buy a different but compatible species.

Selection

When a group of canaries are housed in a flight, the differences between individuals quickly becomes apparent to the prospective buyer.

Taming is also more easily accomplished with young canaries. Older birds may be nervous and frightened for a longer period of time.

Most owners prefer a male since only males will sing. Therefore, they have a higher selling price. The cost will be reasonable, though, since it is based on current competitive prices. A female may sing, but not with the same vigor, and not a continuing, connected song. It will be more like a warble. A male will be loud and lusty, holding himself up. He will be livelier and more bold in appearance. Rely on your dealer to help you determine what sex a canary is. An untrained eye and ear may find it difficult.

If you like color and a good all-around song, then the Color Bred canary is the best and most available in pet shops. They come in a wide variety of colors, from orange, red, white, yellow and so on. The more red in the bird, the more expensive it is. They sing as much as the song canaries, but the voice is not as cultured, more harsh and loud. If you are more interested in a low pitched, beautifully toned singer, then the Roller Canary should be chosen. These are usually available in most pet shops. All male singing canaries, of the pure bred song stock, are kept separated from each other so they may not sing in answer to other birds' calls. If you wish something different and out of the ordinary, investigate one of the type birds. These oddly shaped canaries are interesting for show. Not many pet shops keep these birds on hand, but if you speak to the dealer one can probably be procured.

No matter what kind of canary you choose, always listen to it before purchasing, because each bird differs quite a bit as to song.

A reliable dealer will give a written guarantee, usually up to fourteen days, that the canary you have chosen is a male and will sing. If it does not sing within that time, he will grant you a refund or exchange. He may, at the time of purchase, stamp the wing with an indelible ink to insure that the same bird is returned. This marking will fade and eventually be lost when the feathers are shed during the next moult.

If you intend to breed the bird, choose a female about one year old. Neither bird of the breeding pair should be more than five years old. These birds are in the best condition for mating. It is also important to know the ancestry of the pair. Traits can be passed on that are not displayed in the canaries you have chosen. If you intend to sell the offspring, find out what is the current fancy, canaries of song, color or posture. This way you can be assured of getting a good price.

The primary consideration when selecting any pet is its health. Your canary will be around for years to come, barring unexpected accidents.

Yorkshire canaries staged for competition must each be housed in a regulation show cage.

Selection

Whatever the enclosure, perches for canaries must be a size suitable to their feet.

Cages

Canaries are used to wide-open spaces, so choose a cage with plenty of room. Do not pick a cage on the basis of its being decorative, as it will probably be too confining. This could damage a bird's feathers and subsequently cause a decline in health. The cage needs to be large enough to allow freedom of movement. A good size is about 16 inches (forty cm.) in length for one bird, 20 inches (fifty cm.) for two birds. If for some reason a small cage is necessary, allow your pet daily flights for exercise.

Select a rectangular cage, not round, because these tend to be more cramped. Metal wires, as opposed to wood, reduce hiding places for mites and bacteria and are easier to clean. Vertical wires about three-eighths to three-quarters of an inch apart are close enough to prevent the bird from entrapping its head between them. A few horizontal wires will strengthen the cage and provide a foothold for the canary if it climbs along the sides.

One of the most difficult tasks in taming is moving the bird in and out of the cage. Therefore, the cage door should be large enough for you to remove the bird while it rests on your hand without having to touch any part of the cage. The best doors will swing open, but many slide up. Be careful of this type because they can act as a guillotine if they close unexpectedly on your canary. Secure them with a clothespin or hook. The clothespin can also double as a makeshift perch in the cage or around the house. Some cages even have doors of varying sizes or allow the top to be removed so the canary can enter and exit at will.

Cages typically come with seed and water containers, but plastic or ceramic dishes can be used as well. Place them on the floor of the cage away from any perches to prevent contamination from droppings. There are cages that provide places for dishes to be hung from the side of the cage. This avoids tipping and lessens the chance of droppings ending up in them. It is likely that such a cage will also have individual doors for each dish to facilitate cleaning and refilling.

Canaries feed by cracking open seeds. The shed hulls are dropped back in the dish, accumulate on top of the remaining seed, and need to be removed daily. Some birds cannot find the food underneath the hulls. Seed hoppers can be used instead of open dishes. They have drawers that catch the hulls and can be emptied. This drawer, though, partially covers the seed. Be sure your bird is capable of finding the food when you first use a hopper.

Do not crowd your canary with accessory items. They will clutter the cage, restrict its movement, and distract it from singing. A simple toy, bell, or mirror can be clipped to the cage. Do not use a long string or chain in which a canary can become entangled and injure itself. Table-tennis balls or a branch from a tree can be great fun. Be creative and change the toys periodically. Avoid anything that may be toxic, has sharp edges, or has small pieces that may be swallowed.

If the cage does not come with a perch, select two or three in natural wood. Vary the sizes from three-eighths to three-quarters of an inch in diameter to exercise the bird's feet and legs. Do not place them over food or water dishes, and situate them far enough apart to make the bird fly from perch to perch. A bird must be able to use its wings because exercise is vital for a healthy bird. Make sure the perches are far enough

from the sides of the cage so the tail feathers will not be damaged. One perch high up in the cage will be appreciated by your bird. Allow enough headroom clearance, though.

Line the cage floor with paper towels or plastic. Newspaper print will rub off on the canary and make it look dirty. If there is no bottom grate, a layer of corn cob or the like can be used for extra absorbancy. With a cage grate, sand or gravel paper can be used. The grate prevents the canary from eating the soiled sand and becoming ill. It also keeps the bird from walking in its droppings. Replace this litter every two to three days, or whenever the mess makes you uncomfortable. Some cages have a sliding tray floor that facilitates cleaning. Others

The perch scraper is a handy accessory that makes cleaning perches an easier task.

have a hinged top, or the wire top may be removed entirely and set on a table or floor. The latter is also a treat for your canary if you take it outside. The top can be placed on the grass to let your canary get a taste of nature!

Wash and dry the cage bottom weekly, and periodically wash the cage bars. Scrubbing with a stiff brush will loosen any dried debris. Clean the perches with a brush, fine sand paper, or a perch scraper. Let them dry completely before placing them back in the cage. Wet or damp perches can cause arthritis, rheumatism and colds. The food and water dishes need to be washed daily with hot water and soap. During the thorough cleanings, you might like to have a smaller holding cage available for the bird.

A canary's feather condition directly reflects its diet and the kind of care it receives.

Deciding where in the house to keep the cage is very important. Eye level, about six feet off the floor, is preferable. A cage that is too low may make the canary feel threatened, because in the wild, danger (predatory birds) attack from above. A cage that is too high will deny the bird sufficient human contact. Certainly do not place it on the floor. Hang the cage or set it on a stand or table close to a wall. Having a closed in feeling on one or two sides will make the cage seem more like a nest. The bird will be more comfortable and feel less threatened than if the cage were exposed on all sides.

For the first few days, the cage should be in a quiet room, like a spare bedroom. This is only meant to be temporary, until the bird settles in. After a short time, move it permanently to a more active room. Avoid kitchens where drastic temperature changes are common. Average daytime temperatures should be between 60 and 70 degrees as much as possible. Nighttime can be as low as the high 40s.

Select an area that is free from smoke and well ventilated, but away from drafty windows and doors. Captive birds have a thinner coat of down and so are more susceptible to chills. Avoid heaters and radiators that can be drying, thereby damaging the feathers. Prolonged exposure to warm tempera-

tures may also cause the bird to moult prematurely.

Canaries respond well to sun and light. Expose the cage to a few hours of sun every day, but protect it from excessive heat. Be sure the cage is partially shaded so the bird can protect itself from becoming overheated.

A canary is used to sleeping at sundown. At night, the room should be quiet and dark. If this is not possible, a drape or cloth placed over the cage will do as well. The canary needs its rest. This cloth can also serve to calm the bird should it become noisy, excited or anxious. When it has calmed down, remove the drape. A quiet bird should never be covered during the day.

If you would like to bring your caged canary outside, remember that the cage has high reflective properties. Hang the cage from a tree out of direct sunlight and away from potential predators. It is safe to have the cage on the ground only if the area is free of danger and there is constant supervision. Remember that your bird is a helpless victim and it cannot flee from any harm that may present itself. And never bring a bird outdoors without its cage, no matter how tame it is. Once it flies, you will probably never see it again.

The wire cage is commonly used to house a pet canary. It is durable and easy to clean.

BRINGING HOME

The canary will probably be placed in a box so that you can bring it home. Have the cage, with all its equipment, prepared in advance so that the time your bird spends in the box will be lessened.

During transport, keep the bird warm. The journey will be shock enough, so try to avoid any additional trauma. Moving the bird on a cold, windy, or damp day will increase the chances of the bird becoming ill.

You may want to take the canary to a vet that same day to insure that the bird is in good health. Arrange with the shopkeeper to exchange the bird if the vet says it is unfit. If possible, bring the bird home early in the day to allow it time to adjust to its new home before dark. This also gives you time to re-examine the bird at home after it has had some time to settle in and recoup from the stress of transport. If the bird seems ill or you notice anything unusual, do not hesitate to call the shopkeeper. The longer the delay, the less responsibility will be taken by him. Act quickly if you want a refund or exchange. Do not be alarmed, though, if your bird remains motionless for a prolonged period. It may not eat much for the first few days. This is a normal reaction for any bird that has been moved to strange surroundings. Soon it will relax, move about the cage, and eat heartily.

An untame bird may quiver when it is watched closely. Sometimes a sign of illness, for your new arrival it merely indicates an unfamiliarity with human contact. Approach the cage slowly and quietly at all times. Give the bird time to get accustomed to you.

If you lack experience, you may be a little hesitant to handle the bird. Canaries do not have a painful or harmful bite,

FACING PAGE:
The unusual feathering of the frilled canary results from a genetic mutation that occurred in the course of domestication.

so there is no need to worry. Remember that the bird is more frightened of you. Open the box and place the open end against the cage door. The canary should hop out of the box and into the cage. If it does not move, use a firm but gentle touch to remove the bird from the box. Never grip it by the throat, always support the full weight of its body. Grasping it by the tail feathers will leave you with a handful of tail feathers, but no

A canary in the hand can be inspected carefully for signs of illness.

bird! Wrap your hand around the body of the canary when the wings are in a relaxed position. Place your plam on its back and hold the feathers in place with your fingers. If the bird does happen to fly free, simply capture it with a net or a light towel or cloth. Be careful not to squeeze the bird or wrap it tightly and cause suffocation.

For the first few days, do not attempt to handle the canary. Speak calmly to the bird, but do not create a disturbance. Any sudden movements or noises may alarm the bird.

Bringing Home

Depending on its disposition, the canary may sit quietly or restlessly twitch and move its tail or head. The bird was probably used to an abundance of social contact at the shop, and now it is all alone. Use your own judgement to determine when the bird is ready for more attention and handling. Eventually you may even want to tame the bird. Each canary will respond at its own pace, so give it plenty of time. Do not force the bird to do anything you think is not in its best interest.

Feeding

A balanced diet and plenty of exercise circumvent many diseases and breeding disorders. Diseases have a more deleterious effect on a poorly nourished body, so provide your canary with a variety of seeds and greens.

The basic elements of a canary's diet are water, a seed mixture, and greens.

Because canaries are vegetarians, the seed diet must supply the essentials of proteins, fats, carbohydrates, minerals, vitamins, and calcium. For this reason, a seed mixture is necessary. No one seed is sufficient in supplying the heat and energy materials needed for growth and repair. Commercial canary feed is primarily canary seed, a yellowish seed, round in the middle and pointed at both ends. Because it does not contain a high enough protein content, it is supplemented with rape. This is a small, brownish, round seed. In smaller percentages are niger, poppy, linseed, hemp, lettuce, oats, and others. A commercial mix is preferred because the seeds will be proportioned in a scientific ratio developed specifically for canaries. If you would like to mix your own, it will cost more over time. A common ratio is 35% canary seed, 30% rape seed, and the rest a mixture of "treat" seed in another dish. This treat seed can be found already mixed and available in the store. Any seed given to your pet should be dry, shiny, fresh, and free of dust and dirt.

Gloster Fancy canaries exist in both crested ("Corona") and plain-headed ("Consort") forms.

With Red-factor canaries, the color of the plumage can be intensified by incorporating coloring agents in the diet.

Fresh greens are an important staple in a canary's diet. Local weeds and grasses, not treated with insecticides, are a good source. Lettuce, spinach, dandelion leaves, watercress, celery and peas are easily obtainable throughout the year. They can be secured with a clothespin to the cage bars. Fruits like apples, oranges, and bananas can be cut up and pushed between the bars of the cage for your bird to eat. These are best provided in the morning, then removed before they sour. Do not leave them overnight because they will be spoiled by morning. Wilted, rotten foods are dangerous. A good rule of thumb is to not feed your bird anything that is not as fresh as what you would eat yourself. Packaged, dried greens are also available commercially, but use these only if fresh greens are not to be found.

Egg biscuit, milk-soaked bread, hard boiled eggs and pound cake with butter or peanut butter are other treats for your bird. They should be offered in a separate dish from the regular food to allow it to pick and choose for itself. It may take some time for your canary to accept strange food, but always make it available. Each bird has its own individual tastes. Offer

The exercise of flying helps to keep canaries in good condition.

one new food at a time, and not too often: canaries are sensitive to sudden changes in their diet. All food should be free of dirt and insecticides before offering it to your pet. Never give your bird table scraps! It may become ill or overweight.

A supply of fresh water always needs to be available for your canary. Without it, the bird will die in twenty-four hours. Clean and replenish the water dish every day.

Only a healthy and content canary will sing. A poor diet or improper living conditions are likely to lead to illness.

Children enjoy helping to care for a pet, and the experience is instructive.

Bringing Home

Canaries as diverse in appearance as a Red-factor and a Lizard have basically similar requirements with respect to feeding and housing.

After your bird has calmed down and developed a routine, monitor its food intake over a week. Be aware of how much and what kinds of food it consumes. A canary will eat about 1 ½ to 2 ounces of seed a week. Supply 1 teaspoon daily, more if all is eaten by the next day. In the future, you will be able to note any changes that may indicate disease. During cold weather or while moulting, the bird may eat more in an effort to maintain body heat. At these times, cod liver oil may be added to some of the seed as a supplement. Keep this seed in a separate dish from the regular seed as it is fattening.

It is advisable to establish a fixed feeding routine. Refill the seed dish the same time every day, preferably late pm or early evening when the canary will fill its crop before retiring for the night. The bird will at first pick out its favorite food, then finish the remainder in the morning. Commercial foods are very rich, and your bird's favorite seeds will likely be the most fattening. For this reason, do not be too hasty to replenish its dish. Make sure the bird eats all or most of the seed in order to

The box cage—solidly enclosed on all sides but the front—is the housing favored by those interested in breeding canaries.

get proper nourishment. Otherwise, it may eat too many high calorie seeds and become overweight.

Dealers now offer a variety of containers for food and water that will hold supplies for several days. These automatic dispensers allow you to leave the canary alone for up to three days. In this way you do not have to feel like a slave to your pet.

No more than a three- to four weeks' supply of seed should be kept on hand in order to avoid spoilage. Seal it in moisture-proof containers in the refrigerator or some other cool, dry place. Moisture and humidity may foster molds which will make the bird ill. Also, with time, seed can dry out and lose its nutritional value. Periodically taste the seed. It should be sweet and nutty, not bitter. Another test is to wet the seed and place it on a damp paper towel or some moist dirt. After a few days, if it does not sprout, then it is not a good food dry. The grasses that do sprout are a treat for your bird.

If you follow this routine, there will be no need for special foods, tonics, or conditioners. Your canary will be happy and singing for its lifetime.

Grit and cuttlebone

Grit contains essential minerals and elements for your canary. It is stored in the gizzard as an aid in digestion, especially of seed. The grit, or bird sand, should include charcoal, important in some internal chemical reactions. Ideally, some other organic material, such as oyster shells or barnacles, should be included in the mixture. If it is not, these compounds can be bought separately and added to the grit. Crushed eggshells are a good substitute. The organic materials are especially needed during breeding. Keep the grit in a separate dish and replace it every few weeks, or more often if it becomes soiled.

Cuttlebone is the internal shell of the cuttlefish, a marine animal closely related to squid. It provides calcium for a firm beak, strong eggshells when breeding, and also prevents egg binding. During breeding, its consumption may be doubled. Gnawing on the cuttlebone or a similar mineral block helps to keep the beak from becoming overgrown.

Unprepared, natural cuttlebone is too salty for canaries. Soak it for a couple of days in water. Usually it comes with a clip, but if not, punch holes in it and attach to the side of the cage near a perch with wire.

The outside-bath, hung before the open cage door, is readily accepted by most canaries after a short time.

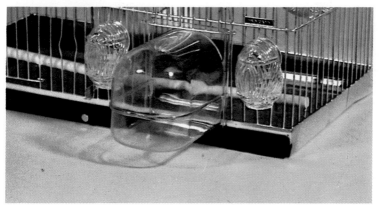

Feather clipping

Clipping your new pet's wing feathers will make taming easier. Taming can still be done without clipping, but it will be considerably more tiring for you and the bird. Clipping the wing feathers means that the canary will have limited ability to fly. It will lose its balance and have to land after traveling only a few feet. When the bird is let out of the cage, there is no possibility of its escaping.

Done properly, wing clipping is quick, easy, and painless for your bird. It can be done by one person, but is easier with two: one holds the bird while the other clips. It is best to watch someone else do it before attempting it yourself. The clipping can be done in the pet shop, which will also prevent the canary from associating a bad experience with its new surroundings.

A group of eight-week-old Border Fancy canaries.

In many canary varieties, like this crested Red-factor, the wing and tail feathers are devoid of pigmentation.

There are two main methods of wing clipping: (1) cutting all the primary feathers, or (2) cutting some secondary and all primary feathers except the outer two or three. The latter method preserves the long, graceful appearance of the flight feathers in the resting position.

One or both wings can be clipped. Clipping only one results in the bird losing control over its flight direction. This facilitates taming because the bird is more quickly discouraged from fleeing when it cannot fly where it intends.

If you choose to clip the feathers yourself, support the body of the bird on your lap or a counter. Never hold it by the neck or the tail. Place your thumb under the lower mandible and your second and third fingers around its head. Keep the neck straight without pushing or pulling the head. Use the other fingers to hold the feet and torso. Monitor the bird's respiration for symptoms of distress.

Extend the wing from the bend to get a clear view. Use a pair of barber scissors or small wire cutters for cutting. Trim no closer than one-half inch from the skin. Cutting along the tips of the covert feathers is a good guide. If you cut a growing feather or trim too closely, bleeding may occur. Having styptic powder on hand to stop the bleeding is a good idea.

Be aware that the flight feathers will be fully regrown in about six months. If you intend to keep the bird clipped, check for new growth periodically. Or you may prefer not to reclip after the bird is tame. It is amusing to see the bird fly around the house and return to the cage at will.

Bathing and preening

In the wild, canaries like to roll in the damp grass. Putting dewey grass or wet lettuce leaves in the bottom of the cage will be a real treat for your bird. A shallow dish of room temperature water, large enough to splash in, will serve to keep the bird clean. After the bath, though, it will be necessary to change the cage bottom. Special bird baths allow the bird to enter, splash about, and shake the water from its feathers, all in a protected enclosure so the floor is not splattered. Many varieties are available at reasonable prices. Other dishes hook on to the outside of the cage, but many birds are afraid of these.

A daily bath should be allowed in the warm weather. Twice a week is sufficient when the weather turns cool, but if the room is cold, do not let the bird bathe. If the bird gets chilled while wet, a cold may ensue. The best time for a bath is early in the morning. This gives the canary plenty of time to dry out before nighttime. Do not leave bath water available all the

FACING PAGE:
Frequent bathing promotes sleek, tight-feathered plumage.

A tame canary may be allowed flight time out of its cage, provided it is supervised by its owner.

time. If your bird won't bathe itself, splash a little water and soon it will get the idea. Don't be surprised if the canary gets itself soggy and dripping wet.

Bathing is particularly important during the moult, as it promotes feather replacement. During breeding, the damp hen will return to sit on her eggs, keeping the egg membranes moist to ease hatching.

After bathing, the canary will preen itself. It will fluff up its feathers and shake them. With its beak, the bird will re-arrange the feathers and put them back in place. At the base of the tail is the uropygial gland from which a small amount of oil will be gotten and rubbed on the feathers. This adds a gloss to the canary's appearance and acts as a natural protectant.

Some tame birds bathe in a sink and enjoy being squirted with the sprayer. It is not unusual for them to fly to the sink when they hear the sound of the water running!

Bringing Home

Taming

Young canaries are tamed most quickly. Older birds are usually more shy. Their taming requires more time and patience. As with any bird, though, the more time invested, the faster the results. Have a family member with plenty of time and motivation do the initial taming. Give short lessons of fifteen to twenty minutes to keep the bird from overtiring and losing interest. Give a taming lesson each time the bird is removed from the cage. Several times every day is suggested. Too much time in between, and continuity is lost. The more accustomed a bird is to human handling, the easier it will be to train further.

At first, the canary may shiver or avoid your advances. Be patient. Allow the bird a few days to adjust and calm down. Speak calmly to the bird and move closer to the cage, making no sudden movements. When the canary pays attention to you, stick or hand taming in the cage can begin. Use your own judgment to set the pace. Each bird has its own temperament.

Canaries, like this just-fledged youngster with its parent, will not be frightened of people if they have had contact with them from the time of hatching.

Remove any unnecessary dishes or toys from the cage. The fewer extraneous items there are, the less distraction for the bird.

Speak and whistle softly to the bird to keep it calm. Offer a perch. Press this stick or your finger into the breast region of the bird to make it climb onto your finger. A bird may respond better to a stick when moving it in and out of the cage. If it attempts to bite, do not make any jerking movements that

The hand-tame canary is quite prepared to perch on its owner's finger.

are frightening. It can also be used as a handy device for retrieving the bird from high places. The bite may pinch, but skin will not be broken. Never hit the bird, just say no loudly. The canary will soon stop. Sometimes the bird may use its beak to steady itself when climbing. This is not intended as a bite.

Once the canary is relaxed on your hand, stroke and scratch it to simulate preening. The bird is now ready for further taming out of the cage.

This canary shows both red and black plumage coloration.

Choose a small quiet room, one with little furniture and no high perches. The fewer things there are for the bird to bump into or hide behind will make retrieval that much easier. Make sure there is no escape through an open window or door. Pull the drapes so the bird will not fly into a window, and cover all mirrors. You may want to have a stand ready outside of the cage to place the bird on after a session.

Scatter a few seeds in front of the cage to entice the bird to come out. If it does not come out on its own, bring it out on your finger or a stick.

A Gloster Fancy canary hen.

Work closely to the floor by getting on your knees. This prevents long falls. If there is no rug, spread out a towel for traction and to cushion landings.

Move slowly and approach the bird from the front. Never sneak up on a canary and grab it from behind. A frightened bird is not trainable. By not alarming it, the bird will relax and soon realize no harm is intended.

Surround the bird from below with outstretched fingers. Now coax it onto your hand. Backing it into a corner may make this easier. Let it perch until calm. Slowly lift your hand from the floor and stand up. This may need to be repeated several times before the bird will remain on your hand. Stroke the bird and praise it. A food reward may be useful. Acknowledge good behavior and ignore anything else.

Offer a finger perch higher than the other hand. Again, press your finger against its belly to make the bird step up. Having it rest on the palm and back of your hand is a new sensation for the canary.

Once the bird is comfortable in your hand, you can coax it to your shoulder. With a rolling motion of your hand, the bird will be forced to step on your shoulder to regain its balance. You may even like to try your head. Just remember, there is no such thing as a housebroken canary!

After a session, place the bird on a perch set up outside the cage. If it moves off, simply return the canary to it. Soon it will remain there.

Return the bird to its cage and offer it plenty of food and water. Your canary will probably be tired and thirsty.

Train the bird for longer sessions each day. It will react quickly to attention. To avoid a one-man bird, introduce other family members once it is tame. Have them feed and play with the bird.

Allowing the canary to come out of the cage for exercise will ensure better health and make it friendlier towards people. The bird will fly around to explore, but will probably come back to you with a little encouragement. Feed a canary only in its cage so it will return there when hungry. Filling a dish with fresh food is very enticing.

The least you should expect from taming is to have the

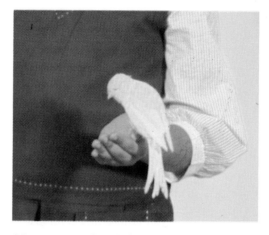

Tame canaries will happily eat seeds from your hand.

canary rest comfortably on your hand. With the bird feeling safe and secure in your hands, it will be easier to examine and treat it in the future.

If you allow your canary to fly around the house, check the flying area for potential hazards. Secure windows and doors and cover the mirrors. Make sure all houseplants are not poisonous to your bird should it chew them.

Think of advanced training as an extension of the initial taming. Use the same room and the same trainer. Short sessions and positive reinforcements of praise and food work best. Do not confuse the bird with too many things at once, and keep them simple. Practice one activity until it is mastered, then introduce another. Pushing toys and climbing ladders can be mastered by a canary. Even natural behavior, like spreading its wings on command, can be reinforced.

Canaries are lively animals, and exercise, especially of the wings, is vital. Even without hand taming, your pet can be permitted to fly about the room. Treated calmly and unhurriedly, it will soon develop a certain amount of trust in its keeper and feeder. This bond can be speeded up by depriving the bird of food for an hour. Leave the cage open so that the bird is free to fly. When you want the bird to return to the cage, replace the food containers in their usual area while the bird is watching. Soon the canary will voluntarily go back to its cage to feed.

DISEASES & FIRST AID

Canaries are remarkably free from disease. A bird that is well fed, properly housed, and kept clean will have little need for medicines and remedies. Under these conditions, canaries will thrive in captivity. Preventive maintenance is, of course, the most important aspect. Accidents and illness can happen, but do not panic. If it is something simple, refer to this book and others, your local sales person, or a vet. For something more serious, be sure to call a vet. Unfortunately, very often a person realizes his bird is sick when it is too late to help. An alert, smooth feathered, bright-eyed bird that sings is healthy.

Note any periods of lethargy and unusually ruffled feathers (in an attempt to conserve body heat). Difficulty maintaining body temperature, respiratory trouble, and a lack of appetite indicate disease. Weight loss can be rapid and fatal.

Isolate sick birds away from all others in a hospital cage. One can be bought, rented, or made by yourself. Cover all but the front of the regular cage, or a smaller one, with plastic or cloth to block drafts and excessive outside stimulation that may excite the bird. A suspended light bulb or a heating pad underneath will provide additional warmth. A constant temperature of 85 degrees is good.

Remove all perches and place the food and water containers on the floor. At this time, your pet may become fussy about the food it eats, so supply some of its favorites. A balanced diet is still preferred, but getting the bird to eat something is most important.

If it is necessary to transport the bird to a vet, keep it quiet and warm. Avoid drastic and sudden changes in temperature.

FACING PAGE:
The author, Anmarie Barrie.

40

Moulting

In the late summer or early fall, your canary will shed its feathers. This is a natural occurrence and will happen yearly. It will take about six to eight weeks to complete. The first year, only the contour feathers will be replaced, not the flight and steering feathers in the wings and tail. All the feathers will be shed from the second year on. This limits the canary's flight and is a strain on the metabolism. Provide a diet high in nutrients, vitamins, and minerals. Balanced preparations are available in the store to promote a rapid and smooth replacement of the feathers. Adding a drop of cod liver oil to some of the seed is a good idea.

You may notice that your canary sings less after each moult. Nothing can be done about this except to check the diet and be sure it is not overly rich, making the bird overweight and lazy.

A moult occurring at an unusual time of the year could be the result of prolonged exposure to excessive heat or improper diet. Keep the canary away from heaters and radiators and check its food.

In the course of a normal moult, feathers are replaced so gradually that no areas of the body are bare.

Leg bands may contribute to injuries which become serious if not treated promptly.

Broken legs and wings

The best idea is to call a vet. Often the injury is more serious than it appears. Broken legs require proper splinting and bandaging for healing. If done incorrectly, the bird may be permanently crippled and unable to breed. A poorly healed wing will inhibit flight. It will take about two weeks for a bird to recover from a break.

Respiratory ailments

Symptoms for a cold are similar to other infections: lethargy and ruffled feathers, possibly accompanied by sneezing, coughing, or wheezing. The bird may have a nasal discharge and sore-looking eyes. If the bird attempts to sing, it may sound hoarse. Typically, this is a result of drafts, dampness, or dust in unclean feed. Try a little honey, iodine, or a 50

43

mg. soluble tablet of oxytetracycline in the drinking water. If the condition persists, call a vet. Not properly treated, the cold can develop into other more complicated and serious conditions, such as pneumonia, asthma, bronchitis, and other chronic and fatal ailments.

Conjunctivitis

Your canary will shut its eyes often and blink a lot. The eyes will be watery. If the condition worsens daily, see a vet for a prescription.

Constipation

The canary will have difficulty passing droppings, which may be small and hard. This is typically the result of an inferior diet lacking in fresh, leafy vegetables. Add greens and and put a drop of castor oil or cod liver oil on the seed. Ripe apple and hard-boiled egg yolk are also recommended. If the condition does not improve after changing the diet, your vet may recommend a laxative.

Diarrhea

Diarrhea is often associated with some other ailment. The canary will sit with ruffled feathers and have a soiled vent from loose, watery droppings. The droppings may also be an unusual color. Diarrhea may result from a change in diet or the consumption of unclean food or water. Usually the diarrhea will stop upon removal of the causative agent.

Remove all fruits and vegetables until the discharge is normal. Offer a dish of poppy seed or some oxytetracycline in the drinking water.

Cuts and open wounds

The bleeding will stop quickly if the damage is not severe. Wash the area with hydrogen peroxide and apply styptic powder. If the injury is more critical, consult a vet.

Feather picking

In this condition, the bird plucks its own feathers, resulting in bald spots. Usually this is caused by lice, but sometimes it is due to a diet lacking in mineral content, so adjust accordingly. Be sure your bird is not anxious or bored. Provide plenty of attention. Also, check the feathers to determine if they are dry, lacking natural oils. If so, add wheat germ oil and wheat cereal to the seed. Move the bird away from any heat source. After a few weeks the bird should stop picking its feathers.

Psittacosis

Psittacosis can be transferred from animals to people. Rare in caged pets, its symptoms in people are similar to pneumonia. If you suspect this disease, see a vet immediately.

Going light

Your canary will exhibit a marked weight loss. Sometimes this is associated with another illness, sometimes the cause cannot be determined. Provide more fattening foods like oats, sunflower seeds, milk-soaked wheat bread, and corn kernels. Your vet may recommend an appetite stimulant.

A Clearcap Silver Lizard Canary.

Heat stroke

Typically caused by a careless owner who left the bird exposed a long time to direct or very strong reflected sunlight. Spray the bird with cool water or rub with a moist cloth or sponge. Chances of recovery are slim if not treated soon enough.

Indigestion

Vomiting is a sign of some other illness or an improper diet. Act accordingly.

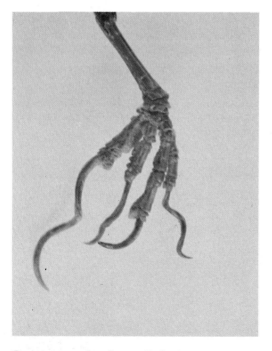

Whenever claws begin to twist, it is a sure sign that they should be trimmed.

Overgrown beaks and claws

Overgrown beaks are rare. They need to be treated very carefully, so it is best to visit a vet. Having cuttlebone and other items for chewing diminishes the chance of occurrence.

Overgrown claws are more common and easily treated. Trim with nail clippers a little at a time to avoid cutting a blood vessel. Treat with styptic powder and hydrogen peroxide should bleeding occur. Smooth rough edges with a nail file.

Trimming the claws is a good idea before mating canaries. Do not attempt to do this during the actual mating time.

Wooden and ceramic perches help to keep claws trim.

Shock and concussion

Usually this is result of an injury such as flying into mirrors, windows, or walls. The canary stops moving and emits crying sounds or it may be silent. The eyes do not focus, and the breathing is shallow. Move the bird to a warm, protected spot. You may wrap it in a cloth and minimize disturbances. Put food and water within reach and check for an injury that may need attention. It may take a while for the bird to respond; meanwhile, leave it to rest.

Try to make the flying area as safe as possible.

Ingrown feathers

These appear as lumps at the base of the feather folli-

The feather lump is large enough to be easily visible among the feathers.

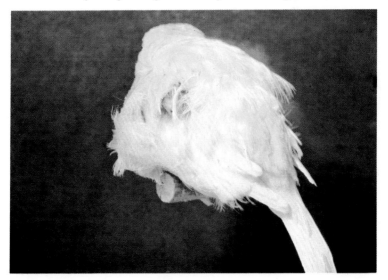

The varying angles and diameters of natural branches exercise a canary's feet.

cles. As the feathers grow but cannot poke through the skin, the lumps grow larger. Have this treated by a vet.

Arthritis, rheumatism and confinement cramps

Often the result of cages that are too small, causing a lack of activity for your bird. Also check for drafts, damp perches, and perches that are too narrow in diameter. Soak the feet in warm water, with some added table mustard, for five minutes. Do not get the rest of the bird wet. Dress the feet with iodine or mercurochrome and leave uncovered. You might like to feed your canary a little olive oil, charcoal, hard-boiled eggs, or some extra vitamin A.

Make sure the bird has plenty of room to exercise, and offer **a variety** of perches in varying diameters.

Diseases and First Aid

Lice and mites

If your bird scratches a lot, closely examine it and the perches. The bird will pick itself, appear puffy, and not sing. Mites live in wood and emerge to feed on your bird by sucking blood or chewing feathers. Lice live in the feathers.

Disinfect the cage and perches immediately. Scrub with a stiff brush and use commercial preparations available in pet shops. The vet will prescribe a suitable treatment for lice on the bird.

Loss of appetite

Typically the result of a change in diet. Although all seeds look the same, the taste varies because they are grown in different parts of the world. It will take a little time for the bird to adjust.

Baldness

Outside of the regular moulting period, check for parasites. Be sure your canary is not being subjected to great fluctuations in temperature.

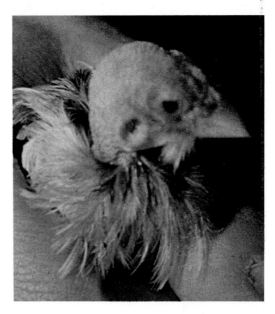

Baldness may have many causes, ranging from dietary and housing conditions to plucking by other birds.

Tumors

Appearing as yellowish lumps under the skin, tumors are often cancerous and result in death. Have them examined by a vet.

Egg binding

Egg binding occurs because the canary's diet lacks sufficient calcium to make eggshells. The eggs are soft and cannot be passed through the vent. The hen will be all puffed up, with eyes half closed. Her breathing will be labored.

Apply two or three drops of mineral oil to the vent and call the vet for further instructions. Attempting to push the egg out yourself may cause it to break inside the bird and cause death. Make sure your pet gets plenty of exercise and a balanced diet.

The enlarged scales on the feet are caused by mite infestation.

Scaly legs, scaly face

This condition is due to a mite that attacks bare areas. On the beak, it causes gray, crusty deposits. It will often go unnoticed, until through scratching the mite is spread to the eyelids, legs, feet, and vent. Afflicted birds may show little initial discomfort, but effective treatment can only be rendered early on. Over time, severe cases of beak deformity can occur, preventing the bird from eating.

Internal parasites

Loss of appetite, weakness, and loose, bloody droppings are symptoms of internal parasites. Their eggs are present in the bird's stool. With microscopic examination, a vet can prescribe proper medication. While the bird is ill, be sure no droppings contaminate its food and water. The parasites will be ingested and the cycle will begin again.

Loss of song

It is not uncommon for canaries to stop singing during the summer months of moulting. If a bird stops singing when it is not moulting, it is a sign something is wrong. Check the droppings and note any respiratory difficulties, illnesses, or injuries.

Most canaries, except the Rollers, sing with open bills.

Breeding canaries can be a time of excitement or of disappointment. Other species of caged birds are easier to mate, although the breeding of your canaries may proceed without a hitch. The entire cycle, from the laying of the eggs to the chicks being independent, takes about two months. Starting mid-March, watch the behavior of the birds.

BREEDING

They will be stimulated by the duration of daylight, not as some believe by the warmer weather.

Determine what type of bird it is that you have; breed for color or singing, not both. Start small and get experience. Past breeders, with skill and patience, have developed the many canary types. Today's hobbyists and pros should live up to their high standards. Refer to other books and speak to local breeders to familiarize yourself with breeding rules and guidelines.

You might like to bring your bird in to a pet shop to ask for a suitable partner. The dealer can select a mate and advise you of some rules of thumb to follow. This needs to be done at least six weeks prior to breeding so the pair can become acclimated to their food and surroundings.

Mating occurs in the spring, so the best time to buy a pair is in December. Throughout out the winter, you can monitor the birds' feed and living conditions. The sexes must be separated and well fed. Males can be kept in rooms of a moderate temperature, but females must spend a cold winter. If they are kept too warm, their mating instinct may be aroused too early. (Chicks reared when there are still twelve hours of darkness may not survive the long night without food.)

One month prior to breeding, the hen should be fed soft foods. This allows her time to adapt to her new diet before breeding. Many commercial raising mixtures are available. These prepared rearing and conditioning foods are more convenient than making a formula yourself. Some breeders do prefer to make their own mixture from eggs, bread, baby cereals, honey, sugar and the like.

Breeding

Be sure both birds are in the best of health and that you have secured a male and a female. Blow the feathers away from the belly and study the area. In a breeding male, the vent is mound-shaped, rising above the level of the abdomen. In a female, it is not so extensively raised. If the intestines are swollen and visible or the stomach is inflamed and red, the bird is sick and not suitable for mating. Males are best recognized by their singing.

Before attempting to build a breeding cage, buy one. This will give you insight for improving on the design. The breeding cage is actually a simple wooden box with a removable wire front or screen. The dimensions should be no less

Canary parents and their two fledged youngsters in the breeding cage.

than twelve inches in length and depth and sixteen inches in height. A tight construction will lessen nurturing areas for mites, lice, and ticks. Within are provisions for feeding, watering, bathing, and hanging a nest pan or tray. A ceramic, metal, or earthenware nesting pan is best. Wicker baskets harbor more parasites. Coat the pan with an insecticide that is harmless to birds, then line it with felt or a similar material. A sliding metal tray will ease cleaning of the cage floor. Fill it with coarse sawdust, wood shavings, or ground corncobs. Fine sawdust is too messy. It scatters and sticks to the birds' feathers. Three perches of various sizes are placed throughout the cage: one each near the food and nest, and one running lengthwise a few inches from the floor. The perches should not be too close to the ceiling because the cock needs room to flutter his wings when copulating. Also, no toys or extra gadgets are to be in the cage.

A double breeder joins two of these boxes together, separated by a removable solid partition and a screen. The partition prevents the pair from seeing each other before both are ready to mate. (The cock is usually ready before the hen.) Use of the screen also allows the male to feed the hen and the young without being able to cause any damage.

The double breeding cage may be divided into two compartments by means of a partition in the center.

Since males are promiscuous and will mate with several females in a season, a treble breeder can be used. A cock is situated in a cage with a female on either side. As the first hen lays her eggs, the cock is mated with the second female. He remains between them to later help with the rearing of both clutches.

Place the birds in a room with maximum privacy and minimum disturbance, such as an attic or spare room. The temperature should be around 60 degrees, not to exceed 70 de-

Canaries nests are not covered, but "open"; this "pan" may be made of various materials, from ceramic to wire.

grees. The pair needs to be caged alone, with no companions. It is impossible to say how long they will need to be kept apart, but they need time to get used to the cage and to one another. If the cock is entered too soon the female may not be ready. She will refuse to mate and fighting may occur.

Soon the male will increasingly sway from side to side with dropped wings. He will attempt to peek around the partition to glimpse the hen. In her absence, the cock may regurgitate and appear to feed his feet or the perch. There will be loud mating calls.

The hen increases her activity, becoming more restless. She will run about, flap her wings, and give a trilling mating call. At times she will crouch low on a perch with her tail raised. Some females may begin plucking their breast feathers. This is the time to give her nesting material. She will build her nest right up to the time of laying, so you do not want to provide the nesting material too soon. Otherwise, she may ruin a nest that has already been built. Nest bags of hay, moss, and cowhair can be bought, or you can provide pieces of cotton, wool, rags, and chopped string. Be sure the strands are short enough that the birds' feet cannot become entangled. At this time, the partition can be removed. The male can then feed the hen through the screen.

The hen's abdomen is now pear-shaped, showing a reddish inflammation near the end. When she sits in the nest and turns about in it, enter the cock the following day. Before transferring, trim his claws so he does not hurt the female when he mounts her. He uses his claws to gain a foothold on the female's back. For heavily feathered birds, trim the feathers around the vent to remove any barrier to fertilization. Once fertilized, the majority of hens can finish the nest, incubate the eggs, and raise the young without companionship. They manage the responsibility well. Males are usually reintroduced when the young are about two weeks old to aid in rearing, but their utilization is not necessary. As a general rule, males are troublesome pests. They break the eggs and sing to the hen to lure her into mating. The males should be altogether out of sight, not just in an alternate cage. If the female neglects the eggs or is a poor mother, return the cock. He may sit on the eggs while the hen feeds, or he may feed her while she roosts. If the female needs to be removed, he will raise the young.

Prior to laying, the female has a lump on the underside of the tail near the vent. She may look ruffled and bloated, and her breathing is more labored. She will lay from two to six eggs, one every one or two days. An average of four to five pale blue eggs with tiny brown specks will be laid early in the morning. The last egg will be slightly darker in color. If mating successfully takes place but no eggs follow, after a week a new hen is required.

Breeding

Dummy eggs (these are made of plastic) in a wire nest lined with a piece of felt.

Remove each egg around noon time and replace it with a dummy egg purchased from your pet shop. Do not touch the eggs with your fingers, for they are very fragile. Use a small spoon, setting them on cotton, cornmeal, oatmeal, wood or sand. Store them at room temperature, turning once or twice daily. They will keep up to two weeks this way.

When the hen has finished laying, return the real eggs to the nest and take away the dummy eggs. Doing this means the chicks will all hatch about the same time. If left alone, they would hatch every few days in the order they were laid. Raising chicks at different stages of development is more tiring for the parents.

While the eggs are being incubated, cease the daily bath and the special rearing food. Consumption of soft food at this time might make the hen want to breed again too soon.

On the twelfth day, provide the bath water as usual. After the hen bathes, she will return to sit on the eggs. Her damp feathers will moisten the egg membranes to ease the hatching of the chicks. If the cock is present in the cage at this time, the hen may not leave the nest to bathe and the eggs will dry out.

Do not disturb the eggs unless for some reason you are suspicious about their fertility. Using a spoon, remove one of the eggs. After four or five days of incubation, fertile eggs will be opaque. Sterile eggs appear clear and transparent, indicating an infertile male.

After thirteen to fourteen days of incubation, the young will hatch. They are born naked and blind. For the next sixteen days, they will be totally dependent on the hen. Do not help them to hatch or you might do some harm. The chicks that do have trouble are weak and best left to die. As they hatch, reintroduce nestling food to the hen. You may like to add some milk-soaked bread, hard-boiled egg yolk, and pieces of apple or carrot. Both male and female canaries regurgitate to feed their young, so do not be alarmed. Since the young have food in their yolk sac, it may seem the parents feed them very little the first few days.

Soft foods can be introduced to the babies on the second day. When the hen sleeps on a perch and not on the young, about the sixth day, the cock can be entered to help with the feeding. Some males will attack the young, so keep a watchful eye.

Around eighteen to twenty-one days, the young will show their plumage. The pin feathers around the face are among the last to develop. The chicks will leave the nest and sit on the low perch. Put a dish of rearing food on the floor to make it accessible. Crush some seed between two sheets of paper with a rolling pin or bottle and add to the mixture. Or soak the seeds for twenty-four hours, drain, and leave on a damp towel for twenty-four hours. At this time, the chicks' beaks are still soft and cannot break the hulls. Hard seed is not offered until the young are six weeks old. They are still dependent on their parents for nutrition. The males will soon sit and sing, while the females do not.

The hen may start to build a new nest for the next clutch. If you plan to breed again, enter the cock and remove the old nest or place it on the floor. Present the hen with a new tray and nesting materials. Be careful that she does not pick the feathers of the young for her new nest, and that the cock does not attack any chicks. It is best to separate the young before mating resumes, although some may help with the next brood. It will be about twenty-eight days before the young are fully independent and can be separated for good. Be sure their beaks are firm enough for hulling at this time. Still provide soft food, because the chicks will not be fully weaned onto dry seed for about forty-nine days. Once removed, keep the sexes separate.

Allow your birds to rear one or two clutches a season. The young should be weaned and ready for the first moult in the fall. They should be about five or six weeks old by then. The parents will also be physically weakened if permitted to continue. The young will not be as healthy, and the parents may not be able to take proper care of them.

Stop breeding canaries after their fifth season. Older birds are not as fit as those one to five years of age.

Hand rearing

Illness or aggression in the adults may require the removal of both parents. Hand-rearing means a great sacrifice on your part. It will cut into the routine of your social life, and hand-raised chicks may not thrive as readily as those raised naturally.

If the chicks have not been abandoned but the parents will not feed them, leave them with the parents and take them out to feed. If the chicks have been totally abandoned and are

Canary nestlings reared by hand may be fed moist, crumbly food on a small stick.

very young, place them in an incubator. For the first four days of life, retain a constant temperature of 102 degrees. Gradually reduce this to seventy degrees. When the birds are feathered enough to retain their own body heat, they can be placed in a cage.

Feed the young every fifteen minutes, keeping one side of the crop full. Moisten some commercial rearing food and offer it on a small spoon or with an eye dropper. Slow this to every hour, keeping the entire crop full during all daylight hours. Wipe the birds' mouths with a damp cloth or Q-tip after feeding. Dried food may cause sores and once crusty will be harder to remove.

Dishes of water and rearing food should be available at all times. Sprinkle crushed or soaked seed on a piece of bread to introduce the chicks to pecking. They will begin feeding themselves in about twenty-one days. Hand-reared chicks may be dependent longer than other chicks.

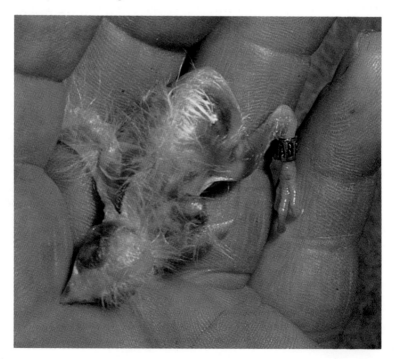

Chicks should be permanently identified with leg bands. If you sell your birds to a pet shop, the only way a dealer will know your birds at a later date is by their bands. Also, it is not possible to enter canaries in an exhibition unless they have been banded.

RINGING

Rings can be ordered through your specialty canary association or club. Many breeders have the bands specially made for their birds with their name, address, code number, and year on them. As a ring is used, record every one in an index file. Any pertinent information needs to be written down because, over time, memories do become faded.

There are two ways to ring the canaries. One is to use split rings, easily slipped onto the young when they are weaned from their parents. They are light weight, colored plastic rings, numbered consecutively. Opened by a special tool, they are placed on the chick's leg.

The other method is to use closed rings, which can only be put on the birds when they are a particular size, about five or six days old. If placed on too early, the band will fall off. If the chicks are too large, the band will not slide over the foot. The canary's foot needs to be taken between your fingers so that the back toe points towards the back and the other toes are stretched towards the front. Grease them with petroleum jelly or salad oil. Bring the front toes together and pass the ring over them, then over the ball of the foot and onto the shank of the leg until clear of the rear toe. Wipe the lubricant off with a soft, dry cloth.

FACING PAGE:
The closed ring (bearing the breeder's initials in this case) can only be slipped over the foot when the chick is a few days old.

SUGGESTED READING

The following books by T.F.H. Publications are available at pet shops everywhere.

ENCYCLOPEDIA OF CANARIES—
by G. T. Dodwell (H-967)

The history of canary keeping introduces chapters on housing and equipment, feeding and general management, and breeding. A discussion of the breeding cycle and the accessories needed by the birds covers the practical side, while genetics, breeding strategies, and management principles deal with the theoretical aspects of canary husbandry. Chapters on further aspects of care (molting, illness and preparation for exhibition) precede accounts of the various breeds, which cover type, color, and song canaries, including those of North American origin.
Illustrated with 48 color and 28 black-and-white photos.
Hard cover, 5½ × 8″, 281 pp.

THE COMPLETE CAGE AND AVIARY BIRD HANDBOOK—
by David Alderton (H-1087)

Already well known for his books and articles on avicultural subjects, veterinarian David Alderton now surveys the whole field of cage and aviary birds. Treating the species by family, he provides current information on the following seed-eating birds: canaries and other selected fringillids; all the commonly available estrildid finches, with details on Zebra and Society finches; many of the whydahs and weaver finches; a sampling of the buntings and tanagers; and pigeons and quails. The psittacine sections, cover Budgerigars, Cockatiels, lovebirds, and their varieties along with a representative collection of other species. Less usual avicultural subjects are species from these groups: barbets, hornbills, toucans, bulbuls, leafbirds, babblers, thrushes, white-eyes, sunbirds, hummingbirds, mynahs, star-

Suggested Reading

lings, crows, and touracos. Each section contains remarks about feeding, general care, and breeding, followed by species commentaries.

Tony Tilford, who has so successfully photographed British and European birds and color canaries and other aviary birds, contributes color photographs to illustrate 167 of the species, breeds, or varieties written about. Opening with a chapter on avian biology, subsequent chapters cover birds as pets and generally discuss housing, feeding, management, illness, breeding, and the genetics of the color mutations. More than 60 drawings and 20 black-and-white photographs help the reader to visualize anatomical structures, the design of aviaries and furnishings, and the paradigms of inheritance.
Hard cover, 7½ × 9½", 160 pp.

EXHIBITING BIRDS—
by Dr. A. E. Decoteau (H-1036)
Written by a nationally known judge, this authoritative introduction to exhibiting and competition covers all aspects of showing birds. It describes how to prepare for a show, how a show is organized, and what to expect on the day of the show. The discussions of the Schedule of Classes and the theory and practice of judging will be helpful both to judges and to exhibitors. The final chapter looks at the standards according to which the different kinds of birds are judged.
Illustrated with 89 color and 62 black-and-white photos.
Hard cover, 5½ × 8", 192 pp.

 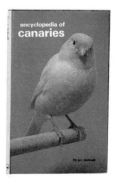

Index